In the Spotlight
Ellen DeGeneres

by Jenna Lee Gleisner

Bullfrog Books

Ideas for Parents and Teachers

Bullfrog Books let children practice reading informational text at the earliest reading levels. Repetition, familiar words, and photo labels support early readers.

Before Reading

- Discuss the cover photo. What does it tell them?

- Look at the picture glossary together. Read and discuss the words.

Read the Book

- "Walk" through the book and look at the photos. Let the child ask questions. Point out the photo labels.

- Read the book to the child, or have him or her read independently.

After Reading

- Prompt the child to think more. Ask: What did you know about Ellen DeGeneres before reading this book? What more would you like to learn about her after reading it?

Bullfrog Books are published by Jump!
5357 Penn Avenue South
Minneapolis, MN 55419
www.jumplibrary.com

Library of Congress Cataloging-in-Publication Data

Names: Gleisner, Jenna Lee, author.
Title: Ellen DeGeneres / by Jenna Lee Gleisner.
Description: Minneapolis, MN : Jump!, [2018]
Series: In the spotlight | Includes index.
Identifiers: LCCN 2018006020 (print)
LCCN 2018001683 (ebook)
ISBN 9781641280396 (ebook)
ISBN 9781641280372 (hardcover : alk. paper)
ISBN 9781641280389 (pbk.)
Subjects: LCSH: DeGeneres, Ellen—Juvenile literature. | Comedians—United States—Biography Juvenile literature. | Television personalities United States—Biography—Juvenile literature.
Classification: LCC PN2287.D358 (print)
LCC PN2287.D358 G54 2019 (ebook)
DDC 792.702/8092 [B]—dc23
LC record available at https://lccn.loc.gov/2018006020

Editor: Kristine Spanier
Designer: Molly Ballanger

Photo Credits: NBC-TV/Kobal/Rex/Shutterstock, cover; sbukley/Shutterstock, 1; Featureflash Photo Agency/Shutterstock, 3; NBC-TV/Kobal/Rex/Shutterstock, 4, 8, 23br; Jason LaVeris/Getty, 5, 23tr; Jason Kempin/Getty, 6–7, 23tl; espies/Shutterstock, 7; Richard Shotwell/Invision/AP/REX/Shutterstock, 10–11, 23bl; Ermolaev Alexander/Shutterstock, 12; Frazer Harrison/Getty, 13; REX/Shutterstock, 14; Dave J Hogan/Getty, 14–15; SAUL LOEB/Getty, 16–17; Jeff Kravitz/Getty, 18; Ian West - PA Images/Getty, 19, 22br; Chris Pizzello/Invision/AP Images, 20–21; Tinseltown/Shutterstock, 22l; Getty Images, 22tr; HaykShalunts/Shutterstock, 24.

Printed in the United States of America at Corporate Graphics in North Mankato, Minnesota.

Table of Contents

Ellen

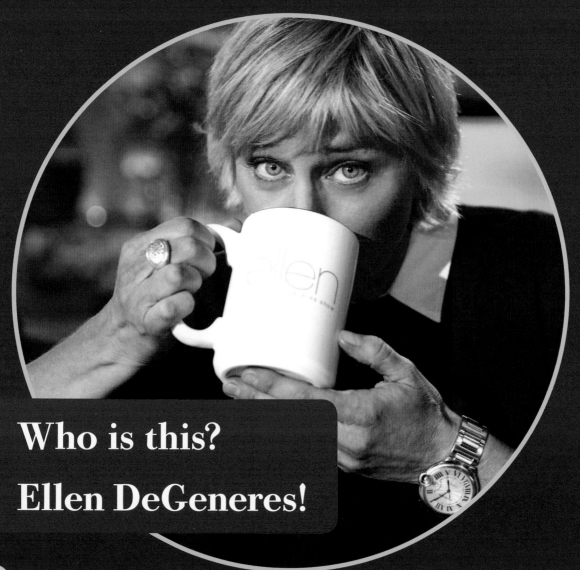

Who is this?
Ellen DeGeneres!

She is famous.

Why?

She loves to laugh.
She makes people laugh.
She is a comedian.

She hosts her own show.
It started in 2003.

She dances.

She does
funny things.

She helps people.
She donates.

11

Ellen loves animals, too.

She helps them
find homes.

13

She has been in movies.

Like what?

Finding Dory!

She is Dory's voice.

Dory

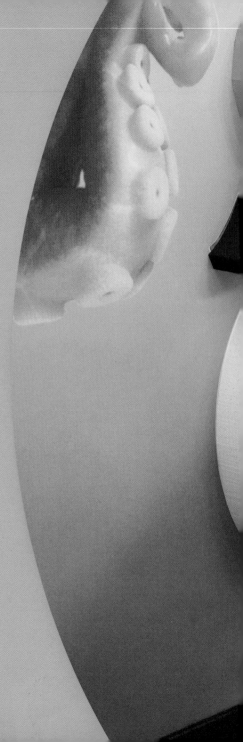

President
Obama

Medal of
Freedom

She won a medal in 2016.
Why?
For being kind.
And hopeful.

Ellen hosts award shows.

In 2017, she won an award.

What was it?

A People's Choice Award.

She asks people to be kind.
Many people like Ellen!

Key Events

January 26, 1958:
Ellen Lee DeGeneres is born in Metairie, Louisiana.

August 16, 2008:
Ellen marries Portia de Rossi.

September 8, 2003:
The first episode of *The Ellen DeGeneres Show* airs on TV.

March 29, 1994:
The TV sitcom *Ellen* airs. Ellen plays the main character.

January 18, 2017:
Ellen wins her twentieth People's Choice Award. This breaks a record for most People's Choice Awards won by one person.

February 25, 2007:
Ellen hosts the Academy Awards for the first time. She hosts again on March 2, 2014.

Picture Glossary

comedian
An entertainer who tells funny jokes and stories to make people laugh.

famous
Very well-known to many people.

donates
Gives something, such as money, to a charity.

hosts
Is in charge of a TV show.

Index

To Learn More

Learning more is as easy as 1, 2, 3.

1) Go to www.factsurfer.com

2) Enter "EllenDeGeneres" into the search box.

3) Click the "Surf" button to see a list of websites.

With factsurfer.com, finding more information is just a click away.